. . . for parents and teachers

Don't Call Me Fatso is the sensitive story of a young overweight girl who questions her own self-worth and competency in reaction to being teased by her peers.

When we meet Rita, she is fearful and feels victimized. It is certainly not easy for a child to be different from other children. Children who are teased and scapegoated because of some difference often *feel* hopeless and powerless — whether they choose to behave passively or aggressively.

I believe this story can facilitate children's awareness of "differentness" at the same time that it models an acceptance of responsibility for a problem and its resolution.

A major value of this story lies in its sensitivity to the sharing of the weight problem and attempts to deal with it within the family. Equally important is the focus on individual acceptance of some responsibility for a problem and for doing what one can about it.

Young children need opportunities to identify with constructive approaches to problem-solving. At the same time, they need exposure to the idea that problems do not always disappear as quickly or in the way we may like them to. Discussing Rita's story can help children to these ends.

BARBARA F. OKUN, Ph.D.
CHAIRPERSON, DEPARTMENT OF
 COUNSELOR EDUCATION
NORTHEASTERN UNIVERSITY
BOSTON, MASSACHUSETTS

Library of Congress Number: 79-23888

  2 3 4 5 6 7 8 9 0 84 83 82

Printed in the United States of America.

Library of Congress Cataloging in Publication Data

Philips, Barbara.
   Don't call me Fatso.

   SUMMARY: Unhappy with herself and the
reactions of others to her, overweight Rita gains
more control over her life as she realizes the
advantages of exercise and healthy eating habits.
   [1. Weight control — Fiction] I. Cogancherry,
Helen. II. Title.
PZ7.P5257Do   [Fic]   79-23888
ISBN 0-8172-1350-3 lib. bdg.

DON'T CALL ME FATSO

by Barbara Philips

illustrated by Helen Cogancherry

introduction by Barbara F. Okun, Ph.D.

RAINTREE CHILDRENS BOOKS

Milwaukee • Toronto • Melbourne • London

Rita and Sue plopped down at a table in the school cafeteria.

Rita opened her lunch box. In no time at all, she finished her peanut butter and jelly sandwich, her marshmallow creme cookies, and her chocolate milk. Then she wrinkled her nose.

"I *told* Mom I hate carrot sticks," she said. "Hey, Sue, I'll trade you my carrots for your cookies."

"Are you blind?" asked Sue. "I just ate some carrots. Anyway, I don't have cookies. My mother gave me a pear instead."

"Well, let's hurry up," said Rita. "It's almost time to go back."

Their teacher, Ms. O'Leary, was waiting for them in the hall.

"Everyone get in line," she said. "We're going to see the school nurse."

Rita walked along with the others to the nurse's office.

"It's time for you all to be weighed and measured," the nurse told them. "We'll do this again from time to time, so we can tell how much you're growing."

Everyone took turns standing on the scale. Soon it was Rita's turn.

She heard someone whisper behind her: "Let's see if Fatso breaks the scale!"

"Be quiet, Allen," Ms. O'Leary warned.

Don't call me Fatso! Rita wanted to shout. But she was too shy to say it out loud.

Then the nurse said, "Seventy-five pounds." He bent down to Rita. "Let's see what your weight is next time. We might want to think about a diet for you."

Rita had already stopped listening. She was the heaviest person in class!

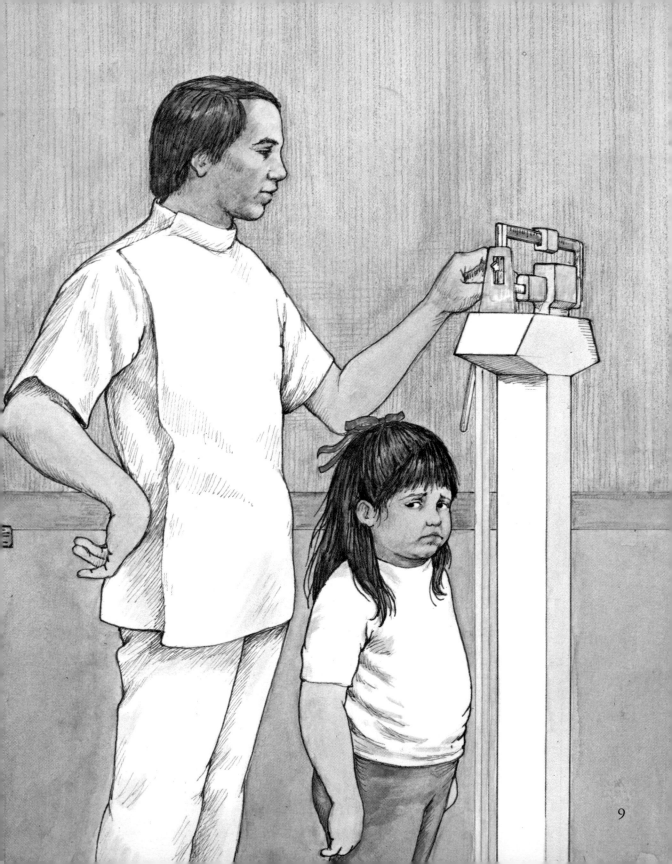

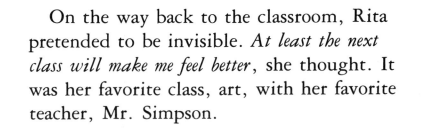

On the way back to the classroom, Rita pretended to be invisible. *At least the next class will make me feel better*, she thought. It was her favorite class, art, with her favorite teacher, Mr. Simpson.

"I want everyone to move your chairs into a big circle," said Mr. Simpson. "Then start drawing a picture of someone in class."

Rita got right to work on a picture of Sue. She didn't even look up when she heard some boys snickering in the corner.

Mr. Simpson walked over to Allen and Mick. "Are you boys finished?" he asked.

They nodded their heads, still laughing.

"We drew Rita," said Mick.

"You mean Fatso," Allen said.

Then they held up their pictures. On each paper were two large circles, with tiny dots for eyes and mouth.

"Don't ever do this again," Mr. Simpson scolded. "People come in all shapes and sizes, and that's no reason to make fun of them."

Rita just looked down at her drawing.

That night, Rita helped her stepfather wash the supper dishes.

"Something wrong?" he asked her. "You're moping around as if you just lost your last friend."

"I practically have! Everyone at school calls me names now, just because I weigh more than everyone else."

"Kids are always making fun of something, aren't they? When I was your age, everyone laughed at my big ears."

"I like your ears," said Rita. "What I don't like is being fat."

"Come to think of it, I could stand to lose some weight too. Why don't we do something about it?"

"You mean a diet?" Rita asked.

"Sort of," he answered. "We could stop eating sweet things and drinking soda pop. And let's stop having desserts all the time. If we're still hungry after dinner, we'll have an apple."

"An apple? But cake tastes much better!"

Her stepfather didn't say anything.

"Okay, I think I get the idea." Rita dropped her dishcloth and ran to her mother's office. "Mom, would you please not put any cookies in my lunch tomorrow?"

Her mother looked up, surprised. "I thought cookies were your favorite part."

"They *were* my favorite part," said Rita. "I don't want to be fat anymore."

"I should lose some weight too," her mother admitted. "We should both get more exercise. Why don't you come jogging with me?"

"Ugh — I mean, I'll think about it, Mom."

17

The following morning, Sue waited for Rita outside the playground gate.

"Guess what!" said Sue. "I'm taking swimming lessons on Saturday mornings now. Do you want to come along?"

Rita started to say no. She liked to
spend Saturday mornings watching TV.
Then she changed her mind.

"Swimming is good exercise, right?
Well, I'd rather swim than jog!"

Rita hated swimming lessons at first.
Putting her head underwater never seemed
like a very good idea.

After a few lessons, she began having more fun.

The day came when she was able to swim all the way across the pool.

"You're quite a swimmer!" called the teacher.

Rita beamed. After that, she could hardly wait for each Saturday morning to come.

One morning the swimming teacher told the class, "Today we're going to jump off the diving board and swim to the other side."

Rita gulped. She was still a little afraid of deep water. When her turn came to jump, she stood on the diving board for a long time.

"Hurry, please," said the teacher. "We don't have all day."

Rita shut her eyes and jumped.

Splash! It felt like half the water in the pool was going up Rita's nose! Coughing and choking, she barely made it to the other side.

As she dragged herself out of the pool, Rita overheard someone whispering, "She's so fat that she sinks when she dives!"

That day Rita bought three candy bars on her way home from swimming. She was finishing the last one by the time she walked in the door.

"What's with you?" asked her stepfather. "I thought you didn't eat sweets anymore."

"Oh, who cares!" cried Rita. "I'm still fat, and the kids still call me names."

"Losing weight takes time, just like learning to swim does."

"But I've been so careful about what I eat."

"I know," he said. "And that's just why you shouldn't quit now — just because things seem hard. You'll feel better about yourself if you keep up the good work."

Rita decided to keep trying. When her friends had ice cream, she had an apple. When they had potato chips and soda, she had celery sticks and orange juice. One day, when Allen called her Fatso, she asked him to stop calling her that.

On the last day of swimming lessons, the teacher spoke to Rita. "You're almost ready for the advanced class. But before I pass you, I have to see you jump off that diving board."

Rita felt sick. Her heart pounded madly as she walked to the end of the board.

I just have to pass, she told herself. *I don't want to stay with the beginners all my life.*

"One, two, three, go!" the teacher counted.

Rita jumped. Without even thinking about it, suddenly she was swimming across the pool.

"You did it," cheered the teacher.
"Good for you!"

And swimming *was* good for her, Rita realized. She kept on taking lessons, and as time went by, she stopped missing sweets so much. Her parents stopped serving potatoes and fried foods, and made big salads instead. They thanked Rita for helping to change the eating habits of the whole family.

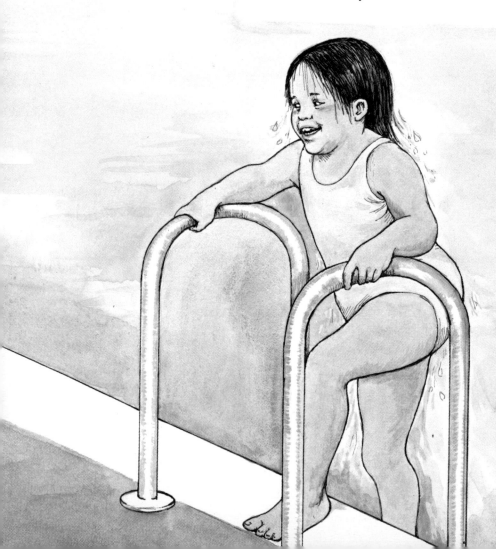

Then came the day that Rita's class went back to the school nurse.

Oh, I hope I've lost weight, Rita sighed to herself. *I never want to be called Fatso again.*

When Rita stepped on the scale, the nurse called out, "Seventy pounds."

Rita almost fell off the scale. "You mean I only lost *five pounds?*" she asked.

The nurse looked at the chart. "But look," he said. "Since the last time I saw you, you've grown more than an inch. You're just fine."

"You really think so?"

"You're as healthy as can be," he told her. "A growing girl shouldn't lose too much weight."

WEIGHT AND HEIGHT SCHEDULE

"Rita! Rita, you're going to be late for art class!"

Rita joined her friends and hurried back to her classroom. She was too busy to notice that no one was calling her names anymore.